BLOOD ON THE HANDLE

BY R. A. MONTGOMERY

ILLUSTRATED BY JEAN MICHEL
COVER ILLUSTRATED BY WES LOWE

CHOOSECO LLC
WAITSFIELD, VERMONT

Book design: Stacey Boyd, Big Eyedea Visual Design

For information regarding permission, write to:

CHOOSECO

P.O. Box 46, Waitsfield, Vermont 05673
www.cyoa.com

Publisher's Cataloging-In-Publication Data

Names: Montgomery, R. A. | Michel, Jean, illustrator. | Lowe, Wesley, illustrator.
Title: Blood on the handle / by R.A. Montgomery ; cover artwork: Wes Lowe ; interior artwork: Jean Michel.
Other Titles: Choose your own adventure ; 33.
Description: [Revised edition]. | Waitsfield, Vermont : Chooseco, [2010] | Originally published: New York : Bantam Books, ©1989. Choose your own adventure ; 94. | Summary: Your only living relative, Uncle Morgan, vanishes, leaving behind a single clue: a jeweled dagger stabbed through the carpet of his study, coated in dripping blood. Your uncle's secrets make you suspicious. Could he be a spy, a jewel thief or something else?
Identifiers: ISBN 1-933390-33-6 | ISBN 978-1-933390-33-8
Subjects: LCSH: Daggers--Juvenile fiction. | Uncles--Juvenile fiction. | Missing persons--Juvenile fiction. | CYAC: Daggers--Fiction. | Uncles--Fiction. | Missing persons--Fiction. | LCGFT: Detective and mystery fiction. | Choose-your-own stories.
Classification: LCC PZ7.M7684 Bl 2010 | DDC [Fic]--dc23
Published simultaneously in the United States and Canada

Printed in Malaysia

12 11 10 9 8 7 6 5 4 3

To Peter Banta and of course, Ramsey.

BEWARE and WARNING!

This book is different from other books.

You and YOU ALONE are in charge of what happens in this story.

There are dangers, choices, adventures, and con-sequences. YOU must use all of your numerous talents and much of your enormous intelligence. The wrong decision could end in disaster—even death. But don't despair. At any time, YOU can go back and make another choice, alter the path of your story, and change its result.

Your parents disappeared on a sailing trip, leaving you alone in the world except for one living relative: your Uncle Morgan. Your life with Uncle Morgan is filled with all of the things money can buy, although sometimes his mansion in New Orleans feels lonely and cold. You're left with some time to wonder about who Uncle Morgan really is—you don't know what he does for a job or how he got to be so wealthy. His friends seem strange, even aggressive. He is surrounded with mystery. One afternoon, Uncle Morgan vanishes. Your only clue is a bloody dagger stabbed through his study floor. Has Uncle Morgan been killed—or was it him wielding the knife? You are alone to solve this mystery—fast!

Your uncle Morgan's house sits, isolated, on top of a small hill in the Garden District of New Orleans, Louisiana. It is spacious and in excellent condition. Your uncle calls it Swan Song.

Your uncle is a bachelor in his early forties and, by profession, a writer and explorer. Besides that, Uncle Morgan is a wealthy man. A very wealthy man. You are his only living relative. Ever since your parents disappeared on a sailboat in the Caribbean six months ago, you have lived with Uncle Morgan in his house on the hill. A cook and a handyman keep things running pretty well. The cook is particularly kind to you. Her name is Maxine, and although she isn't too much older than you, she keeps Swan Song organized and a fun place to be. You're glad she's there, especially since your uncle is often away on trips all over the world.

You get to go away with him on short vacations... sometimes. There is, however, something strange about all of this: the visitors to the house. Although Uncle Morgan refuses to explain why, the visitors are usually foreign. They come either alone or in groups of two, never more than that. They stay a couple of days with your uncle, locked away in his large, book-lined study. Then they leave or, so it always seems to you, vanish. Uncle Morgan usually packs up and leaves shortly thereafter. He doesn't give any explanations.

Turn to the next page.

Once you kidded your uncle about him being a spy. It was the only time you have seen him angry at you. "You must not speak about what you do not know," he told you. "This is all very serious. Maybe even a little too serious."

And yet you have always wondered. You can't help but imagine Uncle Morgan being involved in the mysterious activities that adventure books are written about.

It is early autumn, and the leaves around Uncle Morgan's house are turning colors and starting to fall to the ground.

Go on to the next page.

It is late afternoon, and you are on your way home from school. Being the last person on the bus gives you a creepy feeling. The bus drops you off at the end of an unpaved drive that leads almost a mile up to your uncle's house, Swan Song. Then you are alone. A cool wind comes, and you zip up your jacket and head on up the drive. You sense that something is not quite right: there is a solemnity, a heaviness in the air that tingles your nerves and makes your every footstep seem louder than you would expect. You continue to trudge up the hill, but Swan Song looks cold and uninviting.

Turn to the next page.

4

The first thing you notice when you near the house is that next to Uncle Morgan's Jaguar X358 is a foreign car you have never seen before. Heath, the handyman, is nowhere to be seen, even though he is usually working in the yard at this time.

"Oh well," you say to yourself, "just another one of Uncle Morgan's friends." You push the front door open and enter the house.

"Maxine! Maxine, I'm home," you yell, but there is no welcoming response.

A scuffling sound from the direction of the study attracts your attention. Slowly you approach, reluctant to call out for Uncle Morgan if he is deeply involved in one of his meetings. The hair on the back of your neck stiffens. The door to the study is open slightly.

Advancing slowly, you listen. There are no sounds. No voices.

Turn to page 7.

"Uncle Morgan," you manage in a low voice. "Uncle Morgan, it's me."

No response.

You push open the door to the study. Blood! There is blood splattered all around—on the oak paneled walls, on the yellow sofa, on the floor. In the middle of the room is a large dagger sticking through the oriental carpet, buried in the oak floor beneath. The handle of the dagger shimmers with fresh blood. And there is no one in the room. No one except you.

The dagger is from your uncle's collection of exotic weapons from around the world. You recognize it at once, and a quick sweep of the room reveals the empty spot on the wall where the Nepalese khukuri, with its vicious, curved, tongue-like blade, once hung.

Then you hear it—a car door, no, two car doors slamming. Ducking to the window, you watch as the mysterious foreign car roars off. You think you catch a glimpse of Uncle Morgan's ashen face against the back window. You don't know whether he is dead or alive.

Turn to the next page.

8

Quickly, without taking the time to figure things out, you run down the back stairs and out to the garage. Your uncle's birthday present to you last June was a Kawasaki S2 350. The engine turns over smoothly, and in a spray of fine gravel, you roar down the driveway in pursuit of the speeding car.

The bike accelerates around the sharp corner. You hit 75 miles per hour and lean hard, slowing the bike through the curve, hoping the wheels will carve through the gravelly surface. A fall now would toss you into the pine trees, causing certain injury... or even death.

Turn to page 12.

Sneaking on board the helicopter might be dangerous. You think it might be wiser, and safer, for you to head back to your uncle's house to see what you can find.

You stand alone in the woods as the helicopter clatters off, leaving you beside the road.

You wait several minutes then return the way you came on the motorcycle. Swan Song looks mysterious as you turn up the long driveway.

"I wonder if the cops will be here?" you say out loud, but they are not anywhere around. "Maybe they've come and gone."

"Heath! Maxine!" you call to your uncle's handyman and housekeeper. There is no response. For a moment you seriously consider leaving Swan Song. But you gather up your courage and return to the study.

Turn to the next page.

10

It is just as you left it, with its bloody rug and vicious dagger still stuck in the floor. Carefully, you search the desk, looking for any possible clues to these strange events.

The drawers are unlocked, and the papers inside reveal nothing unusual. You are at a loss to explain anything. Then your eye catches the small marble carving of an elephant that has always fascinated you. It sits on a heavy wooden base. Instinctively, you are drawn to the carving, and you pick it up for closer examination.

You find nothing at first. Persisting in your examination, you focus your attention on the wooden base. It is composed of several layers of fine teak in an intricate pattern. Rubbing your finger along the wood, you hear a click, and a small opening appears!

Turn to page 113.

You realize that it might be best to just follow the man and woman and hope they know what they are doing.

"Hurry. There isn't much time," the woman says.

"Where is the boat?" you ask.

"Main dock. Straight ahead," the man replies as he helps Uncle Morgan, who is having difficulty walking. Moving swiftly to your uncle's side, you put your arm around him for support.

The main dock is covered with canvas, and it muffles the sound of your footsteps. It is an eerie feeling being out here at this time of year, lonely and isolated.

The launch is a 35-foot Cigarette, one of the fastest boats built. Its bright red-and-white striping certainly isn't designed to look anonymous on the water. *What are they planning?* you wonder.

Turn to page 15.

Soon you are at the end of the drive and onto the narrow, two-lane blacktop. It is a difficult series of curves and fall-away corners that is risky at anything above the speed limit. But your speed is coming up on 80 miles per hour! You are now driving by instinct. The car ahead of you is accelerating through the turns, but you push on, gaining slightly.

Then you hear it, the sound of your uncle Morgan's Jaguar. It is right behind you. You quickly check your rearview mirror and see two people whom you have never seen before. One of them holds a weapon outside the passenger window. You have to react quickly. If you try to dodge the car behind you, you may lose track of your uncle Morgan. On the other hand, if you continue your chase, you might get seriously hurt.

If you give up the chase and escape, turn to page 17.

If you accelerate and continue, turn to page 20.

It is difficult getting your uncle Morgan on board, but when he is secure, you quickly busy yourself with the lines casting off.

The powerful twin engines kick into life, and the launch moves away from the dock just as the head-lights of the car enter the yacht club parking lot.

The Cigarette shoots ahead with a surge of power that throws you back into the padded seats. The woman at the wheel powers through the calm water at 40 knots and climbing. The running lights are off.

The high-speed side thrusts you out into the middle of the bay, and there, dead in the water, is a large gray yacht. It too has its lights off.

The Cigarette neatly slides up to this huge, ominous-looking craft. Hands reach down, pulling all four of you aboard.

Turn to the next page.

16

At that very moment, a helicopter descends over the yacht, its searchlights shining directly on you and your uncle Morgan.

"U.S. Coast Guard. Prepare for boarding. Do not move. Repeat. Do not move."

"What's going on?" you shout.

Quickly the men on deck begin dumping packages into the water. You can only imagine their contents.

Two more helicopters arrive. An armed Coast Guard patrol boat pulls up next to your boat, and guards surround you.

"You are all under arrest."

"Don't worry," says Uncle Morgan. "I'll explain later."

The End

You are about to give up your chase and turn onto a narrow dirt path when you feel a sharp, burning pain in your right arm. Your jacket sleeve is ripped along the outer edge; you see a dark gutter of flesh along your upper arm. One of their shots nicked you! The engine on your bike whines, air presses against your body, and the speedometer reads 85 miles per hour. The car with Uncle Morgan in it has disappeared around a curve. Leaning forward, you twist the accelerator handle even harder.

You hear the sound of gunfire again as your tail light shatters. Leaning hard into a curve, you feel the dirt kick up against your leg. "Have to lose these guys," you tell yourself. The road ahead of you divides: the right fork along the bay leads into town; the country road to the left has a maze of turnoffs. Coming out of the curve, you head left for the country road.

The men in your uncle's car are still behind you. Their headlights cast your shadow on the road. The nerves in the back of your neck tighten. You see a dirt road off to the left. This time you will make the turn. Slamming on the brakes, you lean hard to the left, putting the bike almost on its side. You fishtail to a stop, but the car is on top of you. *How did it catch up?* you wonder. Looking up, you see a headlight only feet from your face. You pump the Kawasaki and shoot forward.

Turn to the next page.

The road is narrow. After a few yards the pavement turns to dirt, and trees form a tunnel of darkness. The headlight on your bike beams out over the road before you. A wedge of blackness followed by a window of light moves past you on your left. The car has turned onto the road behind you. But you have a good lead; they can't catch up with you now.

Leaning into the wind, you strain your eyes for possible escape routes. In front of you, two small, bright objects shine out of the darkness. Without thinking you swerve to avoid the frightened skunk that stands paralyzed in the road. Your hand scrapes a tree, throwing your balance off. The bike slips sideways and falls. Somersaulting, you fall between two trees, onto a soft patch of grass. The bike, its headlight a beacon in the night sky, roars on its side in the middle of the road.

Go on to the next page.

Just as the car's headlights shine on you, you turn the bike over and roar off once again. Your heart is racing. The smell of skunk is in the air now, and your eyes begin to water. Your arm still stings from the gunshot wound. You fly past a yellow roadside sign. Then you realize, moments later, what the sign said: DEAD END.

A ledge of white boulders marks the end of the road. You slow down and stop, your motorcycle idling in the cool night breeze. Lights frame you standing alongside your bike. The car approaches and finally comes to a stop. Then you hear the car door open. You wonder if you should wait and see what they want or if you should try to ride away quickly.

*If you stay and find out
what they want,
turn to page 21.*

*If you quickly ride
away, turn to page 32.*

20

Bending low over your motorcycle, you twist the throttle wide open, and the powerful engine accelerates to your command. The bike roars off, the uneven, harsh blacktop road perilously close to you as you power through turns and up and down the rolling countryside.

You are gaining on the car with Uncle Morgan in it. Surprisingly, no one is firing back at you from that car. Easing a bit on the throttle, you back off. *What will I do when I catch them?* you ask yourself. You have no answer.

The noise of a tremendous crash comes from behind. The crash is followed by a muffled explosion, and you see a reddish cloud of smoke and flames in your rearview mirror. The Jaguar has gone off the road. You no longer need to worry about the people following you in that car.

Several cars and a delivery truck pass by in the oncoming lane, and the presence of others on this lonely road gives you some hope and courage. There is a small town up ahead with a country store, gas station, and post office, but it is not a busy spot, and the chances of finding help there are slim. You continue in your pursuit, hoping for the best.

Both you and the car are cruising at about 60 miles per hour, fast for the road but not really dangerous, barring any unexpected obstacles. Suddenly, without warning, the back window of the car opens and a large gray bundle comes flying out.

Turn to page 28.

You decide to stand your ground. *What do these people want anyway?* you wonder. A tall man with a mustache steps out of the car; the other man, the driver, remains behind the wheel.

"You can fight me if you want," the mustached man says, "but I have a gun. It wouldn't be fair, I'm afraid."

"What have you done with my uncle?"

"Get in the car, we'll take you to him," the man says.

You don't have a choice. The man's gun is aimed directly at you. It would be useless to oppose him. He moves away from the car and opens the back door for you. "Come on, get in."

As you start to get into the car, you feel a sharp blow on the back of your head. For an instant you feel pain, then you fall into unconsciousness.

When you wake up, you are on a couch in a storage room of some kind. Your head aches.

Turn to the next page.

You look around and see that the room is filled with old containers of artist's paints and brushes. There is a wooden model, an artist's figure standing on a wooden base, an easel, and several sheets of drawing paper. Some of the papers have sketches on them. The whole place smells musty, like burning candles.

Metal masks hang on the wall. On a workbench, there is an odd, pointed helmet like the ones knights wore in medieval times. In one corner of the room, a suit of armor, missing one arm, stands ready to attack.

There are no windows in the room. When you try the door, you find it is locked. There are voices in the distance. You strain to hear them but cannot make out what they are saying. One of the voices sounds a little like Uncle Morgan.

Turn to the next page.

24

Bending down to peek through the old-fashioned keyhole, you find that your view is blocked. Your captors have left the key in the door. You grab a piece of drawing paper and one of the thin-handled paintbrushes. Slipping the paper under the door, you use the handle end of the brush to work the key out the opposite side. It takes a few tense minutes of work, but at last the key comes free. You hear the clink of metal as it hits the floor. You hope it didn't make too much noise, or worse, bounce off the paper.

Very slowly, you pull the sheet of paper back toward you under the door. There is the key! Peeking out the keyhole, you see several boxes labeled MUSEE CONTI WAX MUSEUM. There are no people around. It looks like it's safe to make your escape. You open the door silently and slip out into the hall.

Go on to the next page.

One glance around tells you that you are in the back storage room of the old Wax Museum downtown. The two loading-bay doors are open. One is empty; the other has a truck backed up to it. A few people are sitting around, as if waiting for something. You hide behind some boxes and watch, wondering what they are waiting for.

Then you hear a sound up in the sky. Lights go on outside beyond the empty bay door. A spiral of dust sprays from the tarmac beyond the truck. The people in the group who've been waiting cover their eyes with their arms. Slowly, a helicopter descends to the ground.

Turn to the next page.

The group that was waiting rushes out to the helicopter and takes several boxes from the cargo bay. They are quick and efficient in their transfer of cargo from the helicopter to a room that is out of your view. *What's in the boxes?* you wonder. *And why are they being delivered to the museum in the middle of the night?*

The pilot of the helicopter climbs out and walks up the steps and into the building. He passes so close that you could reach out and touch him if you wanted. You realize you have seen him before at your uncle's house! Without hesitation, he crosses the room and opens a door that appears to lead to an office. As he closes the door, you glimpse several people inside. Could Uncle Morgan be in there?

Turn to page 30.

You wonder what the man and woman want as you slowly climb off the bike, push it up on its kickstand, and look at them as they calmly wait for you beside the large foreign car. The distance between you and them is about 20 feet; as you hesitate, the woman smiles and beckons to you to join them. Uncle Morgan's face appears in the rear window of the car. His face is devoid of emotion; there is no signal, no clue to help you with your decision.

Hesitantly you step across the moss-covered surface of the bog and head toward the man and the woman.

"Don't be afraid," the man says. "We won't hurt you. We are friends of your uncle's. He wants you to come with us."

"But why...I don't understand...the blood, the shooting?" you stammer.

"Don't worry about the blood. The bullets were a mistake."

"They seemed real enough to me." You bring your hand across to your arm where the bullet nicked you.

"We thought you were someone else. It was a mistake. Come, talk to your uncle."

Turn to page 37.

You hit the brakes, then open the throttle, simultaneously swinging the handlebars through a sharp arc, enabling you to just barely miss the object that sits in the road. Shuddering to a stop, you leap from the motorcycle and race toward the bundle, figuring that it's Uncle Morgan.

The bundle is full of clothes and a seat cushion from the car. They are stained with blood.

You give the bundle a vicious kick and then scramble back on your bike. Once again, you risk your life, speeding recklessly to catch up. But luck is with you. A patch of road construction ahead has slowed traffic, and in a minute you are once again within range of the car.

This time, however, a hand reaches out from the back window, and the red and orange flashes are followed by bullets. One of the shots hits your left rearview mirror, shattering the glass and covering your arm with sharp fragments.

Then the firing stops as the car comes to a stop. The front doors open, and out steps the driver, a well-built young man, and a pretty woman about the same age. They hold up their hands to show you that they are not armed, gesturing for you to come over to them. You're not sure what they want. It might be risky to get too close to them. To the right, there is a side road.

If you risk finding out what they want, turn to page 27.

If you duck down the road, turn to page 38.

Just then, the men return carrying three ornate Egyptian sarcophagi. They load these ancient coffins, made of a rich, dark wood, onto the waiting truck. You're not sure why, but suddenly you have a scary thought—*what if they have killed Uncle Morgan and put him in a mummy case?* While you think about this possibility, the truck engine starts. You don't have much time.

If you hop on the truck to look inside the ancient coffins, turn to page 46.

If you investigate the office of the Wax Museum, turn to page 49.

The car's headlights make the darkness beyond even darker. You will not risk being taken by these guys. The decision made, you crank the gauge and pop the clutch. Your bike leaps forward. In a flash, you pull back on the handlebars. The front wheel lifts off the ground. You slide between two of the white boulders that form the boundary marking the end of the road.

This must be a cornfield, you think, as you feel the shocks banging up and down. Wind whistles through your hair. A shot sounds from behind you, then another. Then silence. They can't follow you now. Breathing a sigh of relief, you turn the motorcycle parallel with the corn rows. You know what you must do: it's time to return to your uncle's house and report this to the police. Up ahead is a shack with a palm painted on its side. You recognize where you are—that shack sits on a road very near Swan Song. You get your bearings and take off for home.

Reaching the entrance to Uncle Morgan's estate, you shut off the engine of your motorcycle. Hiding the machine in a thicket takes only a few moments. From here on out you will travel on foot.

Turn to page 34.

Leaving the driveway, you cut across the lawn, through the small pine woods on the south side. There are lights on in the house. You work your way around to check the driveway. No cars there. Using a side door, you enter the house.

There is a sound of footsteps upstairs. A shudder runs through your body from head to foot.

"This way, quickly!" It is the voice of Heath, your uncle's handyman.

You start upstairs to the study where Heath's voice is coming from, but something in the sound of this familiar voice frightens you.

"What's the hurry? Morgan is long gone by now."

It's Maxine! You never heard her refer to your uncle so informally before.

"We've got a lot to do tonight if this is going to work," Heath says.

"Why shouldn't it work? We've planned it for over a year."

Edging your way down the hall, you step on a loose board.

Go on to the next page.

"What's that?" Maxine asks.

After a moment of silence, Heath says, "Don't worry. Probably the wind. We're both a little jumpy."

"I'll be glad when this is over."

Turn to the next page.

You continue your approach to Uncle Morgan's study. Near the doorway, you stop and listen. There is the sound of crunching gravel outside—a car coming up the driveway. Maybe Uncle Morgan will open the downstairs door and step into the house. Cautiously you pull back the door and peek around the doorframe into the study.

The room is empty!

Heath and Maxine are nowhere to be seen, and the room is clean! Not a trace of blood anywhere. Even Uncle Morgan's dagger is back in the scabbard on display. His whole collection of artifacts looks untouched.

Before you get a chance to look at the papers on your uncle's desk, you hear a car door slam outside. You recognize the sound—it's your uncle's Jaguar! The two men who were chasing you have returned.

The front door opens, and a footstep on the stairs sends a shiver up your back. They're coming upstairs. You look around the room.

Turn to page 42.

Uncle Morgan's face slides back, away from the rear window, and you are left with practically no alternative. Any attempt to escape at this point might be dangerous for you or your uncle.

Moving almost in slow motion, you advance on the car and the two people.

"See for yourself," the woman says, opening the rear door.

Peering inside the car, you look at Uncle Morgan. He gives you a sickly smile of recognition and raises a hand in salute. His white shirt and tweed jacket are stained with blood.

"I didn't want you to get involved," he murmurs.

"What's going on?" you ask, shocked at his condition.

"Get back on your bike and turn around," he says.

"How can I?" you reply. "They won't let me."

"They work for me," your uncle replies, nodding at the man and the woman.

"It would be better if you stayed with us. We could use your help," the woman says.

You're not sure what to do. You've finally found Uncle Morgan, and he looks like he needs your help. But who knows what will happen to you if you go along with them, you wonder.

If you get back on your bike and turn around, turn to page 65.

If you stay to help Uncle Morgan, turn to page 68.

Your instincts for survival advise you to leave at once.

Skidding the bike into a 90-degree turn, you roar down the side road on the right, expecting bullets to penetrate your back at any moment. But nothing of the kind happens.

Go on to the next page.

Slowing down, you come to a stop and turn back to see if you are being followed. In the distance you pick out the sound of a car at high speed going in the opposite direction from you and another coming your way. You turn around and head back to the hardtop road. Uncle Morgan needs your help. But when you reach the road, you are immediately bathed in the harsh white of searchlights.

"Hands up. Don't move. Anything you say can and will be used against you," comes a voice from a loudspeaker.

Turn to the next page.

40

Three state troopers advance on you, their weapons drawn. On the one hand, you're glad that these are the authorities; on the other hand, you're upset with the way they're treating you.

They do a quick search, satisfying themselves that you are not armed. You are then asked to explain yourself.

Never in your life have you talked so hard and so fast and so earnestly. You tell them everything that has happened to you since you came home from school. Uncle Morgan's life may depend on any one of a number of details.

The lieutenant seems to believe you, and he radios in to his superiors for orders. You wait, fidgeting at the delay. The longer you wait, the harder it may be to find Uncle Morgan.

The lieutenant looks up. "Okay, it's a go. Helicopter is on its way," he says.

The lieutenant and his men seem to be through with you. You step back into the shadows of early evening, apparently forgotten by the troopers.

Go on to the next page.

Soon a very large helicopter marked U.S. COAST GUARD drops down in a field next to the road. Two officers in flight gear jump from the craft and join the state troopers, shouting over the sound of the rotors.

You turn around and head back to Swan Song. *There must be plenty of clues to investigate there*, you think. As you walk to your motorcycle, you can't ignore the huge helicopter. Maybe, just maybe, you think, you could sneak on board. There isn't much time. You must hurry if you are going to do it.

If you return to Swan Song to look for clues,
turn to page 9.

If you sneak on board the helicopter,
turn to page 45.

42

Then you notice one of the built-in bookcases is different from the others. It rests against the wall oddly. *It must be a secret passageway*, you think. You pry the bookcase away from the wall. Sure enough, there is a dusty, cobweb-lined passageway into darkness.

The footsteps are closer now; you have to do something. Rushing to the window, you look down. There is a six-inch ledge and beyond that a twenty-foot drop. Leaning out the window, you see the fire escape leading to safety from the next room. If you leave by the window, you will have to walk the ledge to the fire escape. Maybe then you can get away from Swan Song and find help.

If you enter the passageway, turn to page 81.

*If you walk the ledge and find help,
turn to page 83.*

Luck is with you. The pilot and copilot are too busy with the controls to pay attention to the passenger or cargo bay, and the two officers are talking with the troopers. An enlisted man who was left on the helicopter is busy fussing with equipment.

"Now!" you say to yourself, and before you can change your mind, you quickly step from the shadows and climb aboard the helicopter. No one sees you. You retreat to the rear of the aircraft and take a position behind a pile of life jackets, webbed netting, and other gear. There is a little light inside, and you feel that your chances are good at not being discovered.

Snuggled up against the gear, you wait for what seems like hours but is really just minutes. Then the officers, the state troopers, and their lieutenant clamber aboard. A signal is given to the pilots, and the helicopter staggers up into the sky.

Turn to page 51.

46

The truck engine revs up. You hear the grinding of gears as the driver prepares to pull away from the loading bay. You dash toward the loading dock as the truck leaves, and with all your effort you jump, clearing the space between the loading dock and the moving truck.

"Hey kid!" someone shouts.

Too late. You are in the back of the moving truck with the three coffins. You know what you have to do next. In the movies, all sorts of terrible things happen when coffins are opened. But it has to be done; you must know if your uncle is in one of them. You take out your pocketknife and open the blade. With the knife in your left hand, you begin to lift one of the heavy wooden coffin lids. Just then, the truck stops. You hide behind one of the boxes and wait. A door slams, then there is the sound of metal sliding on rollers. The driver is closing the back of the truck!

Slowly the back of the truck darkens. The door is shut. You hear the heavy click of a lock bolt slipping into place. You are trapped.

Go on to the next page.

47

The caskets rattle in the darkness as the truck bumps along the road. *Where is the truck headed?* you wonder. *And how long will you be trapped inside?* Feeling along the bed of the truck, you crawl to a corner away from the coffins. Hiding your knife in your hand, you sit in the darkness and wait.

After a short while, the truck stops. He's stopped for gas. Maybe you can pound on the door and get the gas station attendant to let you out. Then you hear it: the sound of a coffin lid lifting up. A crack of light appears from the inside of one of the coffins.

If you pound on the door for help,
turn to page 55.

If you find out who, or what, is in the coffin,
turn to page 60.

You decide you are not about to leave the Wax Museum. The chances of Uncle Morgan being on that truck are slim, you feel. You may have a better chance of finding him if you look around the museum. If he is here, there is a chance you might be able to help him.

Working your way around the back room, you try to find some way to get closer to the office. There is a door that leads to the Wax Museum exhibit hall; you try the door, and it opens. Inside you find a long, dimly lit room. A full moon shines through tall, arched windows illuminating several suits of armor. When your eyes fully adjust to the darkness, you begin to explore. There are little alcoves along each side of the hall. Each alcove contains an armor-suited figure with weapon in hand. Bright banners hang from the ceiling. You make out a sign that reads KNIGHTS OF OLD. This place gives you the creeps.

You know that the museum office should have an entrance from the exhibit side—if only you could find it! On the wall is what appears to be a control panel with several knobs.

Turning one of the dials, you see the lights go up just a bit. You try another knob, and a sky scene appears on the ceiling—a crescent moon with dark clouds drifting past. The museum display is a giant diorama of medieval times, with wax figures and real weapons.

Turn to the next page.

50

Having gone this far, you try the last knob. Fog drifts out from vents near the floor. It's a museum effect, and you cannot shut the fog off, even though you try. "Must be on some sort of timer," you say to yourself as you set forth again to find the office.

Walking through the room, you feel as if you are being watched. Turning quickly, you think one of the armored figures has moved, but you can't be sure. You wish the fog would stop rolling out of the vents at your feet. Then you hear a metallic sound, like rusty hinges, or like a suit of armor that needs oil.

A glass display case in the corner catches your attention. It is filled with all sorts of ancient weaponry. You hear the sound again. Looking around, you see that one of the suits of armor has moved. Rushing to the display case, you find it locked. Without hesitation, you remove your shoe and break the glass. The alarm sounds. A Celtic leaf-bladed sword gleams in the shadowy light of the moon and fog.

Turn to page 59.

A large body of water spreads out below you. The helicopter remains stationary, hovering about 500 feet above the bay. The crew is searching for boats. They spot several, and finally you swoop down, approaching the first boat.

"What are they hoping to find?" you ask yourself.

Searchlights snap on and illuminate a medium-sized commercial cargo boat. You can't make out what the state trooper, the pilot, and the copilot are saying, but soon the helicopter moves off in search of different prey.

Before long they have found what they want: a large gray oceangoing vessel. It shows no running lights. Snuggled next to its hull is a red and white speedboat.

"Prepare to board," comes a voice over the intercom. It startles you, and your sudden movement almost reveals your position.

Turn to the next page.

The helicopter hovers directly over the gray vessel, a mere ten feet from the deck. The searchlights bathe the entire ship in an eerie glow.

"U. S. Coast Guard. We are boarding you!"

There is no response, no signs of human activity anywhere. Two of the Coast Guard crew descend on a cable. They carry automatic weapons and are protected by state troopers, similarly armed, who have taken positions at the open side of the helicopter.

Before they have a chance to board the vessel, an enormous explosion rips through the midsection of the boat.

The abrupt, sharp hammering of weapon fire surrounds you. A stitching of bullet holes appears right next to you in the thin skin of the helicopter.

Quickly you jump free of the helicopter and land in the cold salt water.

Turn to page 54.

54

The gray vessel is burning but not sinking. You swim toward the red and white launch. Small-arm fire continues. You can't see what is going on. You hear the sound of other helicopters, and you think you see a yacht approaching. You know you've got to get out of the frigid water fast, but you're not sure which craft is safer.

If you climb aboard the red and white launch,
turn to page 112.

If you climb aboard the yacht,
turn to page 114.

You bang on the side of the truck. "Help!" you scream in desperation.

Nothing could be worse than some ancient mummy popping up out of the coffin. The eerie glow from the ancient sarcophagus illuminates the inside of the truck. *What am I doing here?* you wonder. Suddenly you're aware that your head hurts, like someone has stuck a needle in the back of it. A needle! You remember the Nepalese khukuri dagger in your uncle's study. Something about the study—then you remember! That's when the pain began; that's when you were hit on the head! Or were you? You can't remember.

"Help! Is anyone out there?"

It seems to be working. The casket lid is closing. Slowly the darkness is returning. You bang on the side of the truck, weakly, with your fists.

"I think the kid's coming out of it. Get the doctor!"

"The kid's arms moved, doctor. Seems to be coming out of the coma."

"Any eye movement?"

"None."

"This is a good sign, but I wouldn't get my hopes up. Sometimes random nerve stimulus can make the arms move in coma patients. The kid lost a lot of blood."

Turn to the next page.

56

So you're in a coma. But you feel the pocketknife in your hand. And everything in the truck seems real. Maybe you are dreaming. The lid of the mummy case is beginning to open again. Light fills the back of the trunk. You stand and walk toward the ancient coffin. You want to see inside for yourself. Slowly, you move forward. Each step brings you closer to the edge of the casket. The lid is fully raised now, and whatever is inside must be waiting.

The light is so intense that you cover your face with your arm. Lowering yourself to your knees, you lean over the coffin and look in. There is your uncle leaning over looking at you. Behind him a woman in white is holding a syringe. They both smile at you.

"Doctor! Doctor! The kid's awake!"

The End

A loud siren sounds throughout the museum. A suit of armor clanks noisily behind you, as if it has come to life. Grasping the Celtic sword, you swing around to face the enemy.

Surprised, you watch as the figure disappears into a black passageway. You wonder if this could be some kind of trap? Cautiously, sword in hand, you move to the passageway entrance. You fumble along the wall hoping to find a light switch but find nothing.

Suddenly the siren stops. Bright lights come on in the exhibit hall, making the passageway before you seem even darker.

"Stop, thief!" someone yells as several guards rush into the exhibit room.

Any second now the guards will spot you. Then you'll have to explain the broken display case and what you are doing in the museum—questions you don't really have any answers for. But if you follow the suit of armor into the black passageway, you might get to the bottom of all of this.

If you stay and try to explain, turn to page 73.

If you duck down the passageway, turn to page 77.

60

You've come this far, you might as well face whatever is in that ancient mummy case. The coffin lid is now fully open. Gripping your pocket-knife tightly, you try not to scream.

A narrow beam of light shines onto the roof of the truck. Then the body sits up. You close your eyes and wait. There is a rustling sound. Curling up, you try to make yourself invisible, hoping the corpse won't find you.

A familiar voice whispers, "What are you doing here?"

Could it be? "Uncle Morgan, you're alive!"

"Shhhh. Why shouldn't I be?"

"There was blood all over your study. And the knife."

"You saw that, did you? I had hoped that it would have been cleared up before you arrived."

"What's going on, Uncle Morgan?"

Shining the flashlight at one of the coffins, Uncle Morgan bends down and opens the lid. "Look at this."

The casket sparkles with jewels. It is filled almost to the top with diamonds, rubies, and emeralds.

Turn to page 62.

You look at the sparkling jewels inside the coffin, then back up to Uncle Morgan.

"I'm afraid that my handyman Heath killed someone in my study this afternoon," Uncle Morgan says. "This person was trying to double-cross him."

"So Heath is the big jewel thief I've been reading about in the newspapers."

"Yes, quite a surprise," says Uncle Morgan.

The truck jerks to a start.

"What are we going to do now?" you ask.

"Nothing to worry about. The driver is one of my people. Hiding in that coffin was the only way I could get away from that gang of jewel thieves."

"They were holding you prisoner?"

"Yes, probably would have killed me if it hadn't been for Maxine."

It is dawn when the back door finally opens. Maxine, your uncle's cook, stands at the back of the truck wearing work clothes. "We're here," she says.

Uncle Morgan leans out of the truck. "Get the coffins loaded on the plane as quickly as possible."

Outside, you watch as several men load the coffins in the cargo space of a DC-3.

Turn to page 64.

Uncle Morgan puts his hand on your shoulder.

"It's going to be a beautiful day," he says.

"What are we going to do now, Uncle Morgan?"

"Do? Why, take a trip. I think we're ready for a new adventure."

It's good to see your uncle again, but something isn't quite right. As you watch the coffins being loaded onto the plane, you wonder if *Heath* really is the famous jewel thief.

The End

Uncle Morgan smiles when you agree to turn around and head back to the house.

You take one last look, then smile back at him reassuringly.

He winces with pain. You flinch, and the thought of what may happen to him makes it harder for you to leave him. A plan immediately forms in your head. *I'll double back on the low road and pick up their trail again*, you think to yourself.

"Hurry. We haven't time to waste. There may be others," the woman says. They climb into the car, slam the doors, and are gone, leaving you alone by the side of the road.

Once again you are racing on your motorcycle, hanging on as you zoom off down a back road. You only hope it connects with the road that Uncle Morgan is now on.

Turn to the next page.

The road ahead becomes very narrow and soon turns to dirt and gravel. It is heavily rutted from the fall rains, and you will have to proceed slowly. You splash through puddles and skid through thick, clinging mud. You have to keep reaching up to clean the mud from your face. It's hard to see and maintain your balance.

You are losing time, and time certainly seems to be running out.

What is going on? you ask yourself. *What's Uncle Morgan up to?*

Then something clicks into place. Those two people with him seem vaguely familiar. You try to piece it all together. Somewhere you have seen them before, but where? Then you remember— three years ago, they spent the period between Christmas and New Year's at Uncle Morgan's. You didn't think that they were very friendly even then, but then again Uncle Morgan's friends never are.

Go on to the next page.

At last you hit the paved road again. It is dark, and you switch on your high beams. The car with Uncle Morgan is nowhere to be seen. A feeling of despair and failure comes over you.

Driving frantically, you search the road ahead for signs of the car. You miss a turn, and the next instant you smash full force into a large oak.

Three days later, you finally come out of a coma. Your head is swathed in bandages, and your left leg is in a cast up to the hip. You are in pain.

"What happened?"

"You'll be fine," the nurse replies.

You ask about your uncle, but they know nothing. You try to find some comfort in the fact that he hasn't ended up in the hospital, but you're not sure if that is good news or not.

The End

68

"Uncle Morgan, I can't leave you like this," you say. "It's dangerous."

"Come, we're wasting time. We're lucky the car crashed back there. But that doesn't mean we've stopped them or that we're safe. Get in," the man says. You slide in the backseat next to your uncle and slam the door shut.

Within seconds, the four of you are hurtling down the road at high speed.

"What happened?" you ask your uncle.

"Don't worry, I'll be all right," Uncle Morgan whispers.

"Where are we going?" you ask, encouraged by the fact that these people seem to be helping Uncle Morgan.

"We'll talk later. Take care of your uncle. There's a first aid kit back there somewhere. Then keep an eye out for anyone following us."

Go on to the next page.

Sure enough, there is a small but mostly complete first aid kit in a canvas tote bag under the driver's seat in front of you. You take out a large compress and pressure bandage.

Peeling back the shirt from the wound, you see the torn flesh still oozing blood.

Placing the compress against the wound, you wrap the pressure bandage around your uncle. It is awkward and difficult inside the car, but you manage.

The car rattles down a bumpy dirt road. You think you recognize the location—it's the road to the yacht club on the bay. The season is over, and most of the boats, including your uncle's, have been put away.

The road is a dead end, you notice. "If there's anyone out there, we'll be caught for sure," you say.

Turn to the next page.

The car comes to a halt in the yacht club parking lot. Ghostly forms of sailboats swathed in protective canvas against the coming winter stand in their cradles around the parking lot. A light evening wind has picked up, and some of the rigging rattles against the tall aluminum masts.

"Hurry, we haven't much time," the woman says. "They could be here, you know."

"Who?" you ask, but she doesn't answer you. The headlights of a car come over the hill down the dirt road. Someone is still following you.

"Hurry, we've got to launch," the man says. "Let's get out of here."

You know the yacht club, and you could probably find a better hiding place in a boat or one of the work sheds. Although you have gone along with them so far, now might be the time to speak up.

If you go with Uncle Morgan and them to the launch, turn to page 11.

If you press your companions to follow you, go on to the next page.

"They're sure to find us if we go to the launch. Follow me. There isn't much time," you command.

To your amazement, the man and woman agree.

"Okay, okay. Lead on. This better be good or we're dead," the woman says.

They go around quickly to the back and help Uncle Morgan from the car. They support him as best they can, but it is slow work.

Meanwhile you have found the key to the sail loft in its usual hiding place. With a reassuring click, the lock opens, and you go in. The old sail loft is now being used for the storage of several large motorboats.

The *Todo Mio* looms in the darkness in front of you. It is a 53-foot cruiser of old design. You have always admired it. There is a ladder leaning against it, probably left by a ship's carpenter doing repairs.

Turn to the next page.

Scrambling up to the deck, you are dismayed to find that the door to the main cabin is locked. There is a little space for the four of you to hide.

Your ears pick up noise of a car in the parking lot and the more ominous sound of voices and people running.

"I'm afraid it's all over," Uncle Morgan states dejectedly.

"What's all over, Uncle Morgan? What's all this about?" Your heart is pounding. Your eyes are frantically searching for someplace to hide.

Turn to page 74.

You decide to stay and face the guards. Perhaps they'll be able to help you. You lower the Celtic sword to your side. "Thank goodness you're here," you say.

But the guards don't seem to be listening.

"I can explain everything," you say. "It all started when I arrived home from school this afternoon. There was blood all over my uncle's...."

One of the guards interrupts. He has moved in from behind you and grabs the sword from your hand.

"I wouldn't hurt anyone," you say. "I was only trying to protect myself."

"Protect yourself from what?" a guard asks.

"That's what I've been trying to tell you. There was a person in a suit of armor coming after me. I broke the display to get something to protect myself."

"A person in a suit of armor? You expect us to believe that?"

"Yes," you say. "Something strange is going on. I have been shot at, knocked out, my uncle Morgan has disappeared, people are loading things onto trucks in the middle of the night. Everything seems to be different than what it's supposed to be."

"Maybe we're not even guards," one of the men says, and laughs.

Turn to page 76.

"I didn't want you mixed up in this. I've tried hard to keep this part of my life separate from you, but—"

Before he can finish the sentence, the door bursts open, and a harsh foreign voice commands you to come out one by one with your hands in the air.

Go on to the next page.

The woman next to you fires an automatic weapon, and the loft explodes in a deadly swarm of gunfire. Before long, they have set the loft on fire, and you are unable to escape. The mystery of Uncle Morgan will never be solved.

The End

76

A clanking sound draws your attention. The man in the suit of armor walks into the exhibit hall. The guards look at him in amazement.

"That's him!" you yell. "Arrest him."

But the guards don't move.

The man in armor says, "Hold on to the intruder."

The strong grip of the guards tightens on your arm. Now you are in big trouble.

The End

You have to get to the bottom of this mystery and find your uncle. In an instant, you have entered the blackness of the passageway. You move quickly, keeping one hand on the wall for orientation.

You become aware of people talking some-where nearby. Cautiously, you move down the corridor until you see a door, partially open, marked "Egyptian Room." Peeking inside, you see several ancient Egyptian sarcophagi, the same mummy cases you saw loaded onto the truck. A model of the Sphinx, three times as tall as a grown man, stands silent, seemingly watching you. The room is filled with wondrous weaponry, masks, and mystic artifacts of ancient Egypt. The voices, you realize, are coming from behind the Sphinx.

You move slowly into the room. One of the voices sounds familiar—it's Mr. Crick, the museum curator. You feel as if a great weight has been lifted from your shoulders. Mr. Crick knows your uncle. He has been to Swan Song several times to discuss purchasing your uncle's collection of weapons.

Walking briskly, you circle the Sphinx. "Mr. Crick?" you call out.

Mr. Crick and two other men are leaning over an open mummy case on the floor.

Turn to page 79.

Your voice seems to have startled Mr. Crick. His eyes are wide with surprise as you approach. One of the other men pulls something from inside his jacket and holds it loose at his side. The third man turns, and you recognize him as Heath, Uncle Morgan's handyman.

Looking at the sword in your hand, Heath says, "It was you who set off the alarm?"

"Yes," you begin, "but it was an accident…"

Before you can finish, Heath grabs you. "Enough. Crick, tell the guards to call off their search. We've found our intruder."

"Yes, sir," Mr. Crick says.

"Tie the intruder up," Heath says to the other man.

"Heath, what are you doing? You don't understand," you insist.

"No," Heath says, "*you* don't understand. But that doesn't make any difference now."

You are chilled by the coldness in his voice. As you are being tied to a chair, you look into the coffin. It is filled with gems: a rainbow of colored stones that sparkle in the museum light.

Heath smiles. "You've read in the papers lately about the international jewel thief?"

"You?!"

Turn to the next page.

80

"Your uncle caught on, too," Heath says. "Unfortunately for him, he should not have been so clever. Crick and I had a neat little operation. Traveling with your uncle, I could steal jewels and leave the area quickly. Crick could ship them just about anywhere to sell, using the museum as a cover."

"You mean those coffins on the trucks were loaded with jewels?"

"You're very quick. Now your fate will have to be the same as your uncle's."

Then it *was* your uncle's blood in the study. But somehow you feel there is hope. Your uncle was taken away in a car. You saw him.

"Take the intruder away," Heath orders.

Suddenly a spiked flail whistles through the air, catching the arm of the man with the gun. You look up, startled. Your uncle smiles as he lifts the visor of his helmet. There are several men with him, all holding weapons. One of your uncle's men holds Mr. Crick by the arm as another approaches Heath.

You feel a renewed love for Uncle Morgan as you rush into his arms.

The End

Running back to the secret passageway, you step inside, pulling the bookcase closed behind you. In a moment, your eyes grow accustomed to the dark. Stairs descend in front of you. Slowly, you begin to go down them.

Your face brushes a spiderweb and, ducking your head, you swat at the invisible net. In the darkness, you feel something crawling across your forehead. Wanting to scream, you slap at your face, hoping that, whatever it is, it's not poisonous.

The stairs lead to two rooms. You can see that both room doors are closed. A thin line of light comes from inside the room on the left. As you approach, you hear voices. One of them is Heath's.

"When Carnavon gets here, we can load the stuff on the museum truck and be out of here by morning."

You hear the scrape of the sliding bookcase panel behind you. Someone's coming in after you! Without hesitation, you open the door to the darkened room on the right and step inside. Your breathing is so heavy that you fear your pursuers will hear you. You must not be caught.

Suddenly there is a loud, slow scraping sound next to you! You are not alone.

You tense up and keep silent. You do not wish to be discovered. Then your thoughts are interrupted by the sound of the voices next door.

Turn to the next page.

82

"Did you get Morgan's kid?" you hear Maxine ask.

"No, the kid got away."

You recognize the voice of one of your pursuers.

Evidently they've come out of the passage and into the room next door.

"We've been planning this theft for over six months, and you let the kid get away!" Heath exclaims.

"How were we supposed to know the kid had a motorcycle?"

"Listen Carnavon," Maxine said, "we don't have time to waste. Let's get the truck loaded and get out of here."

Turn to page 89.

Even though heights make you dizzy, you step out onto the ledge. You have to get out of the study. Standing on the ledge, you remember all the movies where they tell you not to look down. You look down. You begin to lean forward, but then you catch yourself. You press your hands against the outside wall of Swan Song and begin sliding toward the fire escape.

"Do you think you hit the kid, Carnavon?"

You stop, hold your breath, and listen.

"I don't know. I only meant to scare the kid. I thought the gun had blanks."

"Where's the paper with the address on it?"

"I left it in the van."

"We can get it when we're ready to leave."

You feel the first drops of rain as you listen to this conversation. *Who are these guys? Why are they here, anyway?* you wonder.

Turn to the next page.

84

You decide you have to get that address from the van. Maybe it will tell you something. The rain is falling harder now; you see lightning in the distance. The mossy ledge feels slick under your feet. Inch by inch you move along the narrow path. The rain is falling in sheets, and your clothes are stuck to your body. Your right arm aches a little from the bullet scratch.

The fire escape is only a few feet away when your foot slips and you lose your balance. Falling forward, you grab for the fire escape.

Turn to page 86.

The flat steel railing of the fire escape cuts into your hands. You feel the strength going out of your fingers, feel them losing their grip on the wet metal. You swing your feet wildly, and your foot finds the trellis. You put some weight on it, hoping that it will hold. It does. Holding the fire escape with one hand, you use the other to get a good grip on the old wooden trellis. Safe at last, you begin working your way to the ground.

Testing the old wooden trellis with each step, you work your way down the south wall of Swan Song. Finally you feel safe. But not for long! When you are halfway down, the trellis pulls loose from the building! With a loud crash you fall backward onto the wet lawn. You gasp for breath. The noise will bring the two thugs after you, you are sure. A light comes on in the kitchen. You stand up slowly, testing for injuries. You seem to be okay.

A screen door opens. "Who's there?"

It's Maxine. You are unsure whether to trust her or not. Moving into the shadow of the house, you wait.

Maxine is framed in the light of the kitchen doorway. Heath stands behind her. "Probably just the storm," he says.

Turn to page 90.

As Heath, Maxine, and the other two clamber out the front door, you feel along the frame of the doorway, trying to find a light switch. It's time to confront your companion in this desolate room. But you can't find any switch. Cautiously, you walk toward the center of the room with your arm above your head. There! You feel a string and pull it. Light from a dusty bulb blinds you for an instant. Then you see what was making the noise.

A line of blood leads to a chair where a man sits, tied up and slumped forward. A jagged circular patch of blood stains the front of his gray pin-striped suit. You feel his cold wrist for a pulse. After a moment, you find it. It is weak, but his heart is beating.

Turn to page 91.

The van is parked in front of the garage. You work your way toward it, keeping out of sight, close to the house. Slowly, you open the door on the passenger side. The overhead light comes on, startling you. Sliding into the seat, you hear the hard rain beating against the metal roof of the van. There is a piece of paper on the seat. You open it and find an address written in your uncle's handwriting: 68 Bourbon Street.

The address is on a piece of stationery from the Musee Conti Wax Museum. You know you have to get back to your motorcycle and take some kind of action. But where should you go?

If you ride into town for help, turn to page 95.

If you check out the address, turn to page 98.

You untie the man from the chair and try to help him to the floor. It is Watson Crick, the director of the Musee Conti Wax Museum! Looking around, you see the room is an old office of some kind. You have never been in here before. Uncle Morgan must keep it locked up. You need something to cover this man up, to keep him warm until you can get help. There is a blanket on a couch against the wall. You cover the man and use one of the couch cushions to raise his feet.

His "thank you" comes as a surprise.

"You're awake!" you whisper.

"They left me for dead."

"What have they done with Uncle Morgan?" you ask him.

"They have taken him captive. Your uncle and I have been working together for a long time. Six months ago he agreed to loan the museum his weapons collection. The weapons are rare, ancient, valuable items. It seems your uncle's employees decided to use the cover of the museum to steal the collection and leave the country."

"But what happened to you?"

"I tried to stop them, so they tried to kill me. This is serious. Morgan must verify that the collection is authentic. After the black market buyer is satisfied, they will probably kill your uncle."

Turn to the next page.

"What? I've got to help Uncle Morgan. And we've got to get you out of here."

"No time. They will be leaving as soon as the museum truck is loaded."

"Why the museum truck?"

"It has special compartments for moving fragile items. Besides, if they are stopped, who would question a museum truck moving rare items?"

"I'll get help for you."

Moving to the door, you open it and slip into the hallway. You feel the cool night air on your face. The door to the next room is open. Beyond the room is a double door that is opened to the outside. A large moving truck is backed up to it. This is your uncle's treasure room, filled with rare weapons like the ones in the study. Maxine is busy packing items in bubble wrap while the men load the truck.

Pressing your back against the wall, you begin moving upstairs slowly, one step at a time, keeping your feet to the edge of the steps so they won't squeak.

"How much time do we have?" Maxine asks.

"We're supposed to be at the warehouse on North Audley Street at 5:00 AM," Heath replies.

Go on to the next page.

"That only gives us an hour before our flight to Chile," Maxine says.

"Stop worrying," Heath says. "It will all be over in a few hours."

Once upstairs, you check the clock. It is 4:40 AM. Not much time. You hear the sound of the truck starting and pulling away down the gravel drive. Rushing to the phone, you call an ambulance for Watson Crick. Then you call the police and tell them to meet you at the warehouse on North Audley Street.

"What's your hurry?" a voice says from behind you. Maxine's hand is in her pocket, holding what might be a small gun.

"Maxine! I thought—" It is hard to keep the emotion out of your voice. "Why are you doing this?" you plead.

"You think too much," she says. "Downstairs. Now!"

Slowly you start to move. At the top of the stairs you hop on the banister and slide quickly away from Maxine.

"Stop that kid!" she yells.

Turn to page 99.

The gravel crunches beneath your sneakers as you hurry down the driveway to your motorcycle. Whenever you have needed help, Uncle Morgan has always been there for you. Now, you must get someone to help him.

The rain is heavy in your headlight; the night is sliced into great luminous sheets of water as you speed along the highway into town. Soon you come upon a tree that has fallen across the road, taking a power line down with it. There's no way to get around the inferno. You open your cell phone. No service. You will have to find a telephone and let the police know your uncle is in trouble. But where?

Turn to the next page.

You remember that Mr. Crick, the director of the Musee Conti Wax Museum, lives nearby. Turning back, you see the van emerge from your uncle's driveway. Quickly, you turn off your headlight, pulling your motorcycle off the road. The van passes you, dark figures in the front seat, heading toward the fallen tree. When it is safe, you ride off toward Mr. Crick's house.

A front porch light is lit. You ring the doorbell. A man about your uncle's age opens the door. He is wearing a burgundy robe and holding a book in his hand.

"Aren't you Morgan's kid?" he asks.

"Uncle Morgan is in trouble," you say. "I need to use your phone to call the police."

"Calm down," he says. "Come inside, you're soaking wet."

Go on to the next page.

"There was blood all over his study," you gasp as you enter Mr. Crick's house, "and I saw someone drive away with him. I'm afraid he's in great danger."

"Do you have any idea who these people are or where they might have taken him?"

"I have an address. I think he may be at 68 Bourbon Street," you say.

Mr. Crick looks at you as if he is trying to make up his mind about something.

"Please, we are losing time. I need to call the police."

"Yes, of course," he says. "I'll phone the police while you change into something dry. Over in that guest room, there are some clothes that might fit. Then we'll drive over to Bourbon Street and have a look."

It feels good to be in dry clothes again. When you come out of the guest room, Mr. Crick is dressed and waiting.

"The police are on their way. We'll meet them there."

"A tree has fallen across the road a mile to the north of here," you say.

"We'll swing around on Interstate 10," Mr. Crick says.

Turn to page 108.

Now you have a lead. You decide to check out the address and find out what is going on. You hurry down the gravel driveway to your motorcycle. The rain is falling in sheets. Ominous thunder rumbles in the distance. Lightning cracks nearby, illuminating the surroundings of Swan Song. It seems almost ghostly.

Riding fast, you feel the rain hit hard in your face. You don't want to be late; you fear Uncle Morgan's life may depend on you. He has done plenty of crazy things in the time that you have lived with him, but this looks serious. Blood all over his study. A dagger in the floor. The thought of it all sends shivers up your spine.

You come to Bourbon Street and turn right. This is a busy part of the city. Neon lights shine in tavern windows. 68 Bourbon Street is a small shop, shouldered between two warehouses. A sign on the shop reads MARIE LAVEAU'S.

What kind of place is this? you wonder. You park your bike and cross the street.

Turn to page 102.

Heath appears at the bottom of the long staircase. You hit him with full force with both feet, knocking him down. Without stopping, you are out of the door and into the night.

Behind you Maxine is screaming, and then you hear the sound of shots. Running as fast as you can, you cut across the lawn. In the distance, you hear your uncle's Jaguar start up. They are after you.

Turn to the next page.

100

Your bike's motor catches on the first press of the starter button. You are away before they reach the end of the drive. As you head for town, a police ambulance, lights flashing, passes you, headed for Swan Song. You have to get to North Audley Street before Maxine and the others, in time to save your uncle.

The truck is parked outside the warehouse. In the distance, the sound of sirens fills the morning air. The police are on their way. If you can only keep your uncle alive until they get here. Behind you, Maxine, in your uncle's car, screams around the corner.

Aiming your Kawasaki for the open warehouse door, you shoot inside. Flipping the engine switch off, then on again, makes your bike backfire loudly. The man named Carnavon is holding a knife to your uncle's throat while two other men talk to him. At the loud sound of the engine back-fire, Carnavon drops the knife and raises his hands.

Go on to the next page.

Your uncle's mouth drops open as you ride directly at him. At the last moment, you screech to a stop.

"Hop on, Uncle Morgan!"

In an instant he is seated behind you on your motorcycle.

"Stop them!" Carnavon cries out.

Revving the engine, you head for the warehouse loading dock. There is no time for hesitation. As you approach the dock, you see Maxine standing on the ground taking aim. You hit the gas, and the bike responds. You leave the dock at 67 miles per hour, flying over Maxine's head as she ducks and fires wildly into the morning sky. You feel your uncle's hold on you tighten as you hit the roof of his Jaguar and slide down the back onto the street.

Flashing blue lights blind you as you come to a stop. Police are everywhere.

"Are you all right, Uncle Morgan?"

"Of course I am. How was school today?"

The End

The window of Marie Laveau's is filled with a jumble of odd powders, bones, plants, beads, and knives—voodoo paraphernalia. You remember reading about voodoo rituals in your social studies class. Don't voodoo worshippers believe that they can bring the dead to life? Zombies—that's what they call them. The walking dead.

Go on to the next page.

There is a narrow passageway between the front of the shop and the warehouse. You decide to have a look out back, even though you are frightened. As you move through the tunnel of darkness, you begin to make out sounds from somewhere in front of you. Faint at first, they slowly get louder.

Your heart beats in rhythm with the drums. You see light now shining through the canvas walls of a long tent erected in the narrow space between the warehouses. Shadowy figures flicker and dance on the canvas wall of the tent.

Moving to the edge of the tent, you lie on the ground and roll under the canvas. There is Uncle Morgan on the ground in the center of the tent. Burning candles are all around him; the smell of incense is thick in the air. Two dancers keep time with the drums.

Turn to the next page.

A man dressed in a loincloth, his body and face painted white, holds a chicken over your uncle. Without looking at you, he says, "We have been waiting for you."

"What are you doing to my uncle?" you cry.

Go on to the next page.

Without answering, he cuts the head off the chicken and drips blood over your uncle. Your uncle blinks and opens his eyes.

Turn to the next page.

106

The drums stop. The voodoo priest drops the chicken and retreats into the shop. The bird flaps its wings, scrambling in great circles around the tent, blood spurting from the place where its head once was.

Uncle Morgan sits up and looks at you, surprised.

"What's going on?" you ask, horrified.

"It's amazing you found me," he says calmly.

"What's going on?"

"I'm writing a book about voodoo called Blood on the Handle. This afternoon, I tried this chicken thing in my study. Got blood all over the place."

"That's strange," you say.

"It's a strange book!" Uncle Morgan replies.

Go on to the next page.

"Let's get out of here," you urge your uncle. "This place gives me the creeps."

"Of course," your uncle says. You look into his eyes. Something is wrong. They don't seem to have the liveliness that you remember. Maybe you are just tired.

Before leaving, your uncle selects a variety of herbs from the dusty showcase inside the voodoo supply house. You notice that one of the herbs is called malwort. A note inside the display case: Malwort, a rare Haitian plant used in sustaining animation of the dead.

You suddenly feel cold and clammy. "I'll head on home with the motorcycle, Uncle Morgan."

"I'll be right along," he says. There is a flatness in his voice. His eyes have a dull glow about them.

You ride back to Swan Song, haunted by the name "Marie Laveau's" and tonight's strange scene.

Upstairs you brush your teeth and slip into bed. After a while, you hear the car enter the drive, the door downstairs opening, then the slow, dead, shuffle of your uncle's footsteps mounting the stairs.

The End

The rain has let up. Mr. Crick's car is warm, with soft, comfortable seats. You are exhausted. Nodding your head, you fall asleep.

"We're here."

You open your eyes and look around. You are in the warehouse district just off North Audley Street.

"This is the Ronalds Street entrance," explains Mr. Crick. "There is also a loading dock on the North Audley Street side."

"What is this place?"

"A storage facility for the Wax Museum," Mr. Crick says.

"Where are the police? Shouldn't they be here by now?"

"I would've thought so," Mr. Crick says. "Let's go in ahead without them. I have a gun." Mr. Crick indicates the weapon in his overcoat pocket. "Come on."

You step from the car and approach the entrance.

"Quiet now," Mr. Crick says.

Inside you see a light in an office near some stairs. There are four people playing cards. Maxine and Heath are among them. The other two are the men who chased you.

"This is the right place," you say.

"Good. Now be careful."

Go on to the next page.

Silently you move toward the office. When you reach the door, Mr. Crick motions for you to open it and step inside. Like a team of TV detectives, you throw open the door. Mr. Crick, holding the pistol in both hands, yells, "Don't move!"

Startled, Maxine rises to her feet. No one else moves. Frozen in time, you wait for some reaction.

"I see you caught the kid," Maxine says.

"Someone had to do it," Mr. Crick says.

You look at him. "What is going on here?" you ask.

"Sometimes people get into something and then want out. Your uncle wanted out."

"What does that mean? Out of what?"

"Heath, take the kid up to Morgan's room."

Confused, you are led away by your uncle's handyman, the man who sometimes tosses a ball with you on the front lawn.

"Here," Heath says.

You hear Heath lock the door behind you. The room has one window, high up, near the ceiling. The room is empty except for a giant galvanized tub filled with dry ice. In the middle of the tub is an open pine coffin, Uncle Morgan lying inside.

Turn to the next page.

Mist drifts up from the dry ice. Condensation has formed on the sides of the wooden coffin. You're not sure whether your uncle is alive or not. Whatever he was involved with, you want to believe he was innocent.

Angry, you are determined to escape. It takes all of your strength to push the big galvanized tub across the tile floor, but you are able to block the door.

Go on to the next page.

You lean the coffin lid against the wall at an angle. *Perhaps this will work*, you think. Stepping back, you take a short run up the coffin lid, then dive for the window frame. Almost. The next time, your fingers catch the edge, and you scramble up, using all the strength in your arms. The window is old, painted shut, with dirty broken wire on the outside. Using your feet, you hammer the window open, breaking it into small pieces of glass and wood and wire.

Outside you take a deep breath and begin to run. It seems miles before you reach a telephone booth. Once inside, you pick up the receiver and dial the operator.

"Get me the police," you say. Then you sit down on the floor of the wet phone booth, shaking, as you try to comprehend all that has happened to you.

The End

112

It's hard to scramble up the smooth side of the red and white launch, but you finally succeed and fall, tired, wet, and cold, into the front seat.

That's when you notice Uncle Morgan slumped in the driver's seat! At first you think he is dead, but as you get closer, you realize that he is still breathing.

"Uncle Morgan, Uncle Morgan, it's me. Let's get out of here."

His response is weak. It's up to you, you realize. Pushing your uncle away from the wheel, you slip into the driver's side. Moments later, the two of you are roaring across the bay away from the burning wreckage.

"What now, Uncle Morgan?" you ask.

"Police....get the police...." he whispers, barely audible above the noise of the engine. Then he slumps forward.

Grimly clutching the wheel, you head to the main dock in the small town across the bay. Once there, you will be faced with endless questions to which you know few answers.

The End

Inside the wooden base of the elephant is a tightly-rolled piece of paper with a list of names and addresses written on it. They are all foreign except for two located in New York City. At the bottom of the list is a name and telephone number. You recognize the name as the head of the FBI.

"Is Uncle Morgan an undercover agent?" you ask yourself. You are sure he is, and you are filled with pride. But fear soon replaces pride as the door to the study swings open and a man enters wearing a mask of black silk.

"Hand over the list," he says.

You hand it to him, and to your amazement, he turns around quickly and leaves. You are safe for the time being. But now you are not so sure about your uncle.

The End

Quickly, you climb the boarding ladder to the gray yacht. The fire amidst the ships is burning with a steady orange glow. There are no more sounds of gunfire.

Moving slowly, you enter the aft compartment, a large, beautifully decorated lounge. You sink, exhausted, into an armchair.

That's when the fuel tanks blow!

The End

ABOUT THE ARTISTS

Interior Art: Jean Michel is a Haitian-American writer and visual artist living in New York's Hudson Valley Region with his wife Jessica and his son Diego. His influences range from Edward Gorey and Kurt Vonnegut to David Bowie and John Singer Sargent. He is currently developing a graphic novel trilogy as well as a Gorey inspired children's book.

Cover Art: Wesley (Wes) Lowe has over 20 years' experience as an illustrator and has illustrated for advertising agencies and publishers in the U.S., Canada, and Europe. He works in traditional mediums and also has done digital illustration for various agencies/publishers. Wes has become interested in exploring sculpture as another form of illustration. He is also working on adding 3D illustrations using Maya and SoftImage and is presently working on a children's book with his wife Nancy. He moved from Toronto in 2005 and is now working from his studio on the Sunshine Coast, a short ferry ride from Vancouver, British Columbia.

ABOUT THE AUTHOR

R. A. Montgomery attended Hopkins Grammar School, Williston-Northampton School and Williams College where he graduated in 1958. Montgomery was an adventurer all his life, climbing mountains in the Himalaya, skiing throughout Europe, and scuba-diving wherever he could. His interests included education, macro-economics, geo-politics, mythology, history, mystery novels, and music. He wrote his first interactive book, *Journey Under the Sea*, in 1976 and published it under the series name *The Adventures of You*. A few years later Bantam Books bought this book and gave Montgomery a contract for five more, to inaugurate their new children's publishing division. Bantam renamed the series *Choose Your Own Adventure* and a publishing phenomenon was born. The series has sold more than 260 million copies in over 40 languages.

For games, activities, and other fun stuff, or to write to Chooseco, visit us online at CYOA.com

⫸ → MAP OF ← ⫷ NEW ORLEANS

1 **Garden District**

Known for "gingerbread" Victorian houses.

2 **Musee Conti Wax Museum**

Known for historical New Orleans wax figures.

3 **Bourbon Street**

Known for Mardi Gras celebration.

4 **Marie Laveau's House of Voodoo**

Voodoo shop with psychic readings

JOURNEY
UNDER THE SEA

CHOOSE
FROM 42
ENDINGS

BY R. A. MONTGOMERY

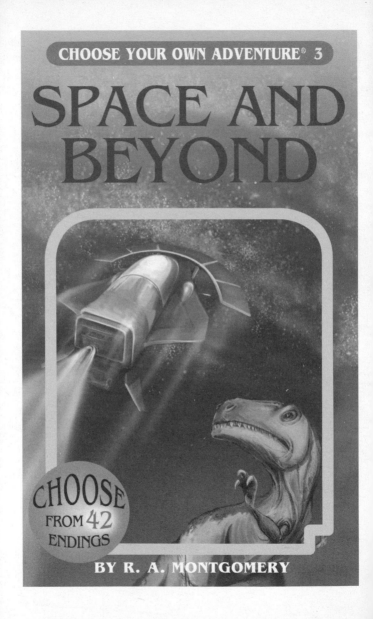

THE LOST JEWELS OF NABOOTI

CHOOSE FROM 38 ENDINGS!

BY R. A. MONTGOMERY

CHOOSE YOUR OWN ADVENTURE® 5
MYSTERY OF THE MAYA
CHOOSE FROM 39 ENDINGS!
BY R. A. MONTGOMERY

HOUSE OF DANGER

CHOOSE FROM 20 ENDINGS!

BY R. A. MONTGOMERY

RACE FOREVER

CHOOSE FROM 33 ENDINGS!

BY R. A. MONTGOMERY

ESCAPE

CHOOSE
FROM 27
ENDINGS

BY R. A. MONTGOMERY

PRISONER OF THE ANT PEOPLE

CHOOSE FROM 28 ENDINGS!

BY R. A. MONTGOMERY

TROUBLE ON PLANET EARTH

CHOOSE
FROM 22
ENDINGS!

BY R. A. MONTGOMERY

WAR WITH THE EVIL POWER MASTER

CHOOSE FROM 30 ENDINGS!

BY R. A. MONTGOMERY

CUP OF DEATH

CHOOSE FROM 23 ENDINGS!

BY SHANNON GILLIGAN

SECRET
OF THE NINJA

CHOOSE
FROM 29
ENDINGS

BY JAY LEIBOLD

THE BRILLIANT DR. WOGAN

CHOOSE FROM 20 ENDINGS!

BY R. A. MONTGOMERY

RETURN
TO ATLANTIS

BY R. A. MONTGOMERY

FORECAST FROM STONEHENGE

CHOOSE
FROM 16
ENDINGS!

BY R. A. MONTGOMERY

INCA GOLD

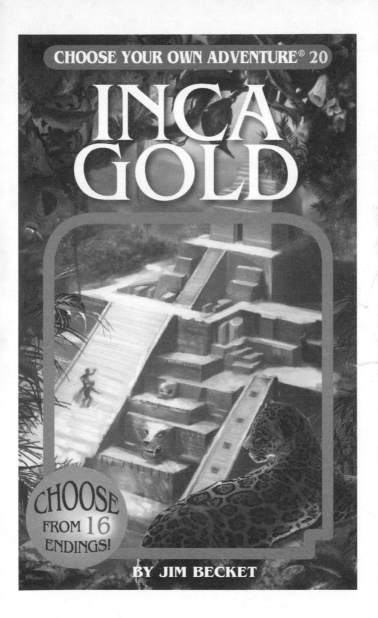

CHOOSE FROM 16 ENDINGS!

BY JIM BECKET

BLOOD ON THE HANDLE

This book is different from other books.

You and YOU ALONE are in charge of what happens in this story.

There are dangers, choices, adventures, and consequences. YOU must use all of your numerous talents and much of your enormous intelligence. The wrong decision could end in disaster—even death. But don't despair. At any time, YOU can go back and make another choice, alter the path of your story, and change its result.

Your parents disappeared on a sailing trip, leaving you alone in the world except for one living relative: your Uncle Morgan. Your life with Uncle Morgan is filled with all of the things money can buy, although sometimes his mansion in New Orleans feels lonely and cold. You're left with some time to wonder about who Uncle Morgan really is—you don't know what he does for a job or how he got to be so wealthy. His friends seem strange, even aggressive. He is surrounded with mystery. One afternoon, Uncle Morgan vanishes. Your only clue is a bloody dagger stabbed through his study floor. Has Uncle Morgan been killed—or was it him wielding the knife? You are alone to solve this mystery—fast!